One Hundred Tips

To

Love Your Life!

By Nicky Marshall

With love,

Nicky

x

www.nickymarshall.org

To Phillip:

Thank you for being dangerous!

To Ami and Kassi:

Thank you both for being perfectly you!

To my family, friends and helpers:

Thank you for encouraging me on this amazing path and for giving me support while allowing me to be my wacky self!

Tip#1:

Give in!

Acknowledge that your plans have changed. Take three deep, level breaths, focus on your body and relax every muscle. Then work out the next three things you need to do to get back on track!

Tip#2:

Have human moments!

We all strive for perfection, spend hours trying to be better and wanting to change something about us.

This is all great but sometimes we get it wrong. On such an occasion, recognise you are actually in a body at this time and therefore mortal, then allow yourself that human moment and laugh!

Tip#3:

Look for the positives!

When something 'bad' or disruptive happens we are so focused on it that we fail to notice the other good things going on around us.

When life throws you a curve ball find one unrelated positive thing to focus on for a few minutes. When you then get back to thinking about the 'bad' event you will also see the positives this has thrown up, for example an opportunity to change.

Tip#4:

Ask!

We all have an internal dialogue that happens as instinctively as breathing. If we are trying to create something or change it is part of that internal dialogue with all the positives and negatives and our brain has great fun worrying us with past experiences or fears.

If we do something external, like writing a letter or taking one action this steps away from our gatekeepers and allows universal law to play.

Tip#5:

Open your eyes.

There is a beauty and energy surrounding us constantly, silent signals showing us the abundance and opportunity of life.

We all have a choice; we can wake up and immediately concern ourselves with our 'to do' list, or take an extra minute, become conscious then look out of the window and observe the possibilities of the Universe.

Tip#6:

Shake it up!

Every day we are bombarded by worries, criticisms, tasks, fears…a host of energies that can attach themselves to us and influence our day.

Find the internal warrior that effortlessly sweeps them away - laugh, dance, interact with soul friends, be inspired and connect with nature.

Nothing negative can exist for long if you fill yourself daily with positives.

Tip#7:

Be unconditional.

There is a little voice inside of us that asks, "What about me?".

Some people have a quiet voice, others you meet have a voice that shouts! As often as you can, do something for someone else, without expecting praise or a gesture in return, just because you choose to.

Sending this thought or act out into the universe will create a gift for you to receive, just when you need it most!

Tip#8:

Believe.

The world we live in is full of elements that we can't see with our eyes… electricity, the air we breathe and, of course, magic!

I believe magic to be coincidence, luck, wishes and intentions.

Today, rather than looking at how you will achieve something, create a clear vision in your mind of what it will look like and allow the magic to do the rest!

Tip#9:

Be real.

We are spiritual beings but we also have a human side. This usually shows up when we are fearful or stuck.

Magic happens when we use our human side to take the next logical step to improve a situation, allowing our spiritual self and the laws of the Universe to see where we want to go.

Today, think of a change you want to make and take one step towards it.

Tip#10:

Be grounded.

We spend so much time using our minds and emotions - thinking or worrying - that we forget we have a body!

Take three deep breaths and send some energy down to your feet and into the earth. Feel that you are attached and ask your body if it's happy…the answer may surprise you.

Wear red socks or nail varnish to remind yourself to be on the planet and aware of your body, then your spirit can float!

Tip#11:

Who are you?

We are all given labels in our life: mother/father/friend/partner. Every day we step into roles depending on where we are and who we are with.

In the morning take a few minutes to really look in the mirror, look deep into your eyes and see that spark…'I am me, I am spirit, I am unique. No one else can do what I can do.' Wow!

Tip#12:

Take control.

We live in a world that thrives on busy-ness, surrounded by technology and a constant buzz of background noise.

During the day take time to come back into yourself, breathe deeply, feel roots that go deep into the earth and a thread that attaches you to the Universe.

Enjoy this focused state for as long as you need. If you are easily distracted by life set your mobile with a reminder — it works!

Tip#13:

Imagine!

For most of us every day arrives without us giving it any thought. This means that we haven't sent any energy into our future.

Before the weekend spend some time thinking of what you will do and be playful - add in some imaginary amazing things and see yourself giggling at surprises and wondering at opportunities.

Send happy, adventurous thoughts forward ready for you to step into. Magic happens!

Tip#14:

Avoid perfection!

When we strive for perfection we focus on a future time and tell ourselves today is not enough.

We are exactly where we should be right now and those 'imperfections' are the perfect lessons for us.

No need to struggle, just choices to make.

We can now see our amazing world, people that love us and an opportunity to make a huge difference to our lives and those around us — how exciting!

Tip#15:

Reinvent your day!

If there's something negative that you say, re-invent it!

Tell yourself that you LOVE everything, it's GREAT when plans change as it adds excitement and change.

Small language changes tell your mind you are having a good time, your mind will then look for actions to back this up and notice any positives that happen.

Enjoy!

Tip#16:

Be inspired!

Sometimes we get stuck - we can't sleep, we are ill, or we are just plain fed up!

Usually other 'bad' events will then join the party and we end up official doom magnets. Have a happy strategy; an inspiring picture, a favourite book, a friend who will sympathise and gently make you laugh…

Make up your own prescription of things that you love and use a 'down' as an excuse to indulge in happiness!

Tip#17:

Are you listening?

Is there something you need to do? Is there something you need to stop doing?

Is your soul quietly singing to you, gently reminding you that there is a better, easier, happier route than the one you are walking today.

Spend one minute today being quiet, tuning in and listening…what does your soul ask you to do?

Tip#18:

Be mischievous!

As children, every day was an opportunity for laughter, we saw the fun in the simplest of things and so pleasure was easy to find.

When we live in an 'adult' world, task and duty are easy to find and, if we allow it, our world can be full of obligations.

Today find the fun: tell a joke even if it's from Google! Search YouTube for something that makes you laugh until you cry...I double dare you!

Tip#19:

Look backwards!

We live our lives through experiences; some make us laugh, some make us cry, but all make us who we are.

It's good to look over our shoulder to see where our footsteps have been.

Through all our experiences there is nothing yet we haven't survived. Rather than dwelling on the past though, allow the teachings to take you forward feeling stronger, wiser and more willing to live the adventure!

Tip#20:

Make choices.

When we choose to do something the energy around us shifts based on our actions.

If we dither and procrastinate, nothing moves and we feel stuck.

Today choose: say 'yes' or 'no' with decisiveness and feel the clarity and freedom that comes with choice!

Tip#21:

Be present.

What proportion of your life is spent worrying about the future or thinking of the past?

How much of your energy is being thrown into the future or is stuck in the past?

The only place you can control now is now, so see all your energy as golden or silver threads and wind it all back into the present. Now every action you take will have power in it!

Tip#22:

Say 'thank you'.

Life is fast these days, with demands on our time from family and friends to work and obligations.

Days can go up and down on a 'by the minute' basis and we can get lost on the rollercoaster.

Pinpoint the good bits - those moments when someone makes you laugh or you realise you are glad someone is in your world.

Today, perhaps as an experiment, thank someone who has added something to your life.

Tip#23:

Are you breathing?

Of course you are as you are still alive, but check to see if you are taking full, deep, breaths that reach down into your belly.

Maybe you only have time to take three deep breaths three times a day but even this will add to your energy, clear your mind and give you time to focus.

Remember small steps climb mountains!

Tip#24:

Be silent.

Have you ever got to the point when you don't know what to do for the best, or been trying so hard you reach utter frustration?

Step back, be silent and observe.

Also listen, for within that silence is the sound of peace and once you tap into that peace you will be able to hear when an angel or helper is around, whether they have wings or are just someone at the end of the phone.

Tip#25:

Change happens.

The natural world is constantly changing, everything is continuous.

When change happens in our lives we can ignore it, fight it or complain about it but it will still happen eventually.

What if we recognised change as an opportunity for adventure?

To clear out all the old and flow with a new energy, to recreate ourselves and the world around us - now wouldn't that be fun?

Tip#26:

Take a snap shot.

In times of busy-ness and change sometimes it's hard to remember our goals, why we wanted to change in the first place.

Go back to a time before the changes and remember how you felt.

If you felt stuck or unhappy think about how you feel today. Even small steps show the universe we are on the path of change.

Tip#27:

Infect everyone with a smile!

Atmospheres and facial expressions are catching, so too is body language.

Walk around with a spring in your step and a smile on your face no matter how good or bad your day is.

Others will follow suit — or want to know your secret!

Tip#28:

Do you hurt?

If you have an ailment or an aching muscle, refuse to acknowledge any problem.

Visualise yourself healthy and happy and if a thought pops into your head about it, simply tell yourself it's not there.

Thanks to Deb Hawken for this great tip, I use it all the time!

Deb Hawken: www.dancing-star.org.uk

Tip#29:

Feel light.

From watching the news or reading a newspaper we can learn about suffering, hardship and sadness.

This can weigh us down, as well as our own busy lives and make us feel heavy.

As an exercise, first feel that your feet are rooted into the ground, then visualise your whole self filling up with fizzy, light energy, as if you could float off at any moment!

Tip#30:

Fill your life with colour.

A flower, a crystal, a vibrant painting or a happy photograph – all these things fill our lives with colour and energise our chakras.

Put something on your desk at work, by the kitchen sink or in the bathroom and when you pass it really look at the colours and feel them blending into your aura.

Tip#31:

Expand!

Whether sitting at work or in a car we all get into postures that make us stiff and our energy shrinks.

Once a day, stand up and stretch upwards and outwards feeling as large as you can.

Imagine that your energy can fill the whole room. Then take three enormous breaths and feel the energy come flooding into your lungs.

Tip#32:

Use both sides of your brain.

We are all predominantly left or right brained and the tasks we do every day will exercise one side more than the other.

Pat your head and rub your tummy, listen to music, do some sums…use both sides intermittently to give your brain a workout!

Tip#33:

Gain a new perspective.

Once in a while challenge your beliefs.

If you feel you have to do something a certain way or at a certain time, ask what would be the worst thing that would happen if you didn't?

Once you realise there are a lot of things that you don't actually have to do, life becomes instantly quieter!

Tip#34:

Accept blame.

When something goes 'wrong' our minds instantly search for a reason why it can't be our fault.

Our human tendency is to blame someone or something else.

If we accept that situation and any part we played in getting there, we can also own the amazing way we handle it, take the lessons with us and honestly own all our 'right' choices too!

Tip#35:

Be bold!

There may be something you are trying to achieve, a dream or an item on your 'to do' list that you have been avoiding.

Even the smallest item can scream loudly or we can blame ourselves for putting things off.

As Goethe said, 'Boldness has beauty, power and magic in it'. So, be bold and get one thing done today!

Tip#36:

Get x-ray vision!

If you think how many things we do, say, hear, think, feel, touch, smell, taste and see every day it's incredible, but perhaps overwhelming?

If today you can take just one moment to step out of the whirl and slow your mind, relax your body and breathe, you may be able to really observe what it is you are aiming for and whether you are on the right track.

Then, consciously adjust your aim as necessary.

Tip#37:

Love yourself!

Loving others is easy, but do you love yourself?

Before you shower your affections on others, first give yourself some praise.

Rejoice in your own talents, love all your imperfections, hug your challenges and spoil yourself every day.

Loving life starts with loving you!

Tip#38:

Imagine.

Every day, before you prepare for work or start looking after others, take your mind off on a journey of imagination.

Imagine a day of smiling people, of easy decisions and happy working.

Imagine effortless relationships and remember to add in one amazing surprise coming your way.

Breathe in the energy of the day and open your eyes smiling!

Tip#39:

Pour in love.

When times are challenging or emotional we lock things away 'to deal with later'.

Over time we ignore it, but the emotions become scary.

We put it off but it nags at us.

Rather than dealing with the whole thing, every day imagine unlocking a drawer, opening it a fraction and pouring in love.

One day you will find the time is right to open the drawer fully and there will be nothing there to deal with!

Tip#40:

Relax.

Completely.

When we are busy we spend so much time in our heads we forget we have a body.

So today while reading this ask every muscle in your body to relax. Start at your toes and work up to your head, feeling all the tension melting away down into the earth.

Take three deep, slow breaths and feel all that energy filling your lungs. Feel that you are right where you need to be at this moment.

Better?

Tip#41:

Is something stuck or bugging you?

When something takes your attention all your energy focuses that way.

When something doesn't work the way you want it to or quickly enough it seeps into your day, your mood and your energy.

Write a letter that is for your eyes only, list all of your frustrations and then very clearly state what you want to happen. Burn it, bury it or shred it — then forget about it!

Tip#42:

Take a snapshot.

Sometimes it takes a birthday or an anniversary for us to do this, but life changes in a moment.

Think back to Christmas last year, last summer, last spring - what has changed?

We are programmed by the news and media to look for bad events, but scan for all the good things that have happened, the challenges you have overcome and those times that made you giggle. Life is for loving!

Tip#43:

Be perfect!

Knowing that you are exactly where you are supposed to be, learning what you need to learn allows you freedom.

Be perfect in yourself right now, whether you are smiling with friends, enjoying your family...or shouting at traffic, worrying over details, eating too much chocolate, slouching or ignoring the ironing. I love this kind of perfection!

(Additional tip: there is no such thing as too much chocolate!)

Tip#44:

Pass on a compliment.

Our eyes are constantly observing, but maybe we keep it all in.

If you admire someone then tell them, if you see something pretty show a friend.

By saying out loud that you appreciate life, life will appreciate you.

When you receive that compliment today, don't dismiss it, say thank you as it's your sign that life has noticed you back!

Tip#45:

How do you sleep?

Do you snore, gnash your teeth, have nightmares or fitful sleep? Do tensions build up by day and come out at night?

Before bed lay quietly and tune in to your body.

Ask your body to relax. Calm your mind and tell yourself any worries will wait until morning.

Write down worries that come up now… or during the night. Then curl up and smile at the lovely rest you are about to have.

Good Night!

Tip#46:

Have you counted your blessings lately?

Thank you Naomi for this inspiring phrase: "I am focusing on the abundance in my life not the lack."

Every day we work towards something, but how about taking time today to appreciate what you have and what you have already achieved?

Naomi: iam_n_maddogg@hotmail.com

Tip#47:

Allow Busy-ness.

Our world today focuses on stress as a bad thing and you can read any number of articles about what it can do to you.

Have you ever experienced the happy buzz of being busy doing what you love?

Bring that feeling into the now, whatever your plans are in the future be happy today knowing you are contributing to your life experience, unique and perfect.

Tip#48:

Get that Friday feeling!

We all know the feeling, when all that working is nearly done and the weekend lies ahead.

Or the day before a holiday with the promise of relaxation and fun.

Today feel the excitement tingling up from your toes, feel the anticipation and the flutter of excitement in your tummy.

Allow a smile to spread across your face because you just can't wait!

Keep that feeling - for every day!

Tip#49:

Learn to switch off.

Sometimes we push ourselves and our bodies because we have a busy period, we are having a social time or we are working towards a project.

We enjoy a challenge and to push ourselves, we release adrenalin and endorphins and have lots of energy.

Just remember to keep this to a defined time and when it's over kick back, relax and give yourself a rest!

Tip#50:

Where there's a will there's a way.

Life may not always run smoothly, but we are surrounded by a network of support.

Whether that's our family, our friends, information on the internet, or signs from nature.

Change may not happen as easily as we want it to and there may be sacrifices, but anything is possible and miracles do happen!

Tip#51:

Today is a present.

Whatever happened in the past brought you to today.

Whatever happens in the future will be influenced by today.

Use today to bring in changes, appreciate what is and connect with others around you.

Why not start something new, act differently or decide to wear new underwear - anything that makes you smile!

Tip#52:

Never give up!

If you have a dream, keep it alive by giving it your attention.

Paint a mental picture and share it with friends and loved ones.

If you get a setback take a day to breathe, then get back up and work out what it is you are missing in your puzzle.

Ask to be given that piece…and remember miracles happen!

Tip#53:

Random acts of kindness.

Sometimes life takes a high speed turn and a few days can easily roll into one.

We can become preoccupied with being busy and time can fly.

At times like these look out - there may be someone on hand to show you some kindness, tell you they love you or just ping a text to say they care: priceless!

Tip#54:

Soak up the sunshine!

For an instant feel-good spend 5 minutes outdoors.

Stand in the sunshine, close your eyes and feel the sun's energy flooding into your core.

See yellow sun-filled energy filling up every part of you.

See your solar plexus (this is the chakra at the base of your ribs) expanding with feel good vibrations.

Listen for birdsong and maybe stand under a tree, allow nature to nourish you.

Tip#55:

Have you ever marvelled at the human spirit?

In times of adversity or challenge there is a huge outpouring of strength, ingenuity, focus and speed that allows the most meek of people to do amazing things.

Everyone has super powers and the ability to endeavour when challenged.

You are capable of anything and the Universe can provide the support needed to assist you.

Go for it!

Tip#56:

Who are the inspiring women in your life?

Friends, partners, family, authors, colleagues.

Use today to thank the women that have inspired you and also praise the men that are in touch with their feminine side!

I love the phrase, 'Behind every man is a strong woman.' We don't crave limelight just love, respect - and chocolate! xx

Tip#57:

What simple thing in life gives you the most pleasure?

To be happy is sometimes perceived as hard or unattainable, but as an adult have you ever been on swings?

Or tried to hula hoop?

Or led on your back in warm grass and watched clouds?

The simpler the better!

Tip#58:

Allow illness.

Sometimes even the most healthy of people can get a sniffle, or have an off day.

If today is that day then allow it, go slower, be kind to yourself and sympathise with your body.

By refusing illnesses you stack them up ready for them to come out the next time you go on holiday or relax.

Why not give in just for today and tuck up with any free time you have.

Tip#59:

Give up!

In life we try to be independent and make up our own minds, fight our own battles and support ourselves.

Sometimes though when it all gets too much it's ok to shout for help.

That person may not have all your solutions, but they may say something to point you in the right direction, or just make you laugh and take your mind off the problem for a while!

Tip#60:

Where do you go to be inspired?

When you are tussling with something find a blank piece of paper and write down all you thoughts.

Go for a walk in woods, enjoy an evening with friends or listen to your favourite music.

With a smile on your face and a song in your heart return to your paper and notice how you see things differently!

Tip#61:

Every day is a new day.

A new dawn, a new opportunity.

Whatever you did yesterday, today is an opportunity to change, to do things differently and take a new path.

If you don't fully manage it don't be down-hearted as another new day happens tomorrow.

Use today as a day of transformation, see beauty, connect with others with an open heart and love the possibility of life.

Tip#62:

Has anyone ever said anything about you that was untrue?

Did it sting at the time and when you think about it does it make you feel uneasy?

It doesn't matter what anyone else thinks, as long as you know you did your best at the time with what you knew then stand tall.

Write: "I have nothing to regret about..." and see what comes out, then burn it, shred it or bury it and feel instantly lighter!

Tip#63:

Do you have a dream or wish?

If it was possible to achieve it tomorrow are you physically fit?

Do you have the energy reserves to make it happen?

Are you in the right frame of mind to enjoy it?

Today build a reservoir, a small tank of energy that is kept back, just for you.

Guard it, protect it and don't give it to others, being kind starts with being kind to yourself, so make a deposit today!

Tip#64:

Listen to what you tell yourself.

The conscious mind has no sense of sarcasm, if you say your feet are killing you that's what it believes.

Listen to the language you use and change it.

Say out loud how refreshed you feel after sleep, how satisfied you are after a meal and how amazing your life is.

Your mind will then spot all the times that back these facts up, allowing you an easy, happy and healthy life!

Tip#65:

Do something that scares you!

In life we get into our 'safe zone', having a routine that is familiar.

When we get an opportunity to do things differently it raises uncertainty and sometimes fear.

Expand your sphere of influence by saying yes to something that scares you, then change the fear into excitement.

Once it's done your world will be a bigger place and your confidence will have increased!

Tip#66:

Wait.

When something challenging happens our brain springs into action running scenarios based on our past.

Instead wait...for 30 seconds.

In this silent gap you will find peace, calm and maybe some inspiration from your guides.

If nothing else you will notice that you are still breathing, life still goes on and that you are safe.

The next step you take will be more positive and possibly even brilliant!

Tip#67:

What do you know?

So often we rely on what others tell us to decide about ourselves, like whether we are capable of doing something or trying something, or whether we are happy.

Our instinct is to ask the opinions of others before we listen to our own voice.

Today before you send that text or e-mail pause…you may be surprised to know you already have the answer!

Tip#68:

Are you present?

How many times have you driven somewhere and not remembered your route?

Have you been walking back to your car and forgotten where you parked?

Today be present, aware of everything you do.

Smell the air and feel your feet on the ground.

Better?

Tip#69:

Have you felt how amazing it is to smile lately?

To completely smile so your whole face lights up and your heart literally feels like it will burst because it's so full of love?

To experience that complete feeling of wellbeing and the sense of being alive?

If not then watch the sunset, grab your absolute favourite DVD, arrange a night with your best friends...or sit and remember your best day ever - so far!

Tip#70:

Do it!

Today find someone to thank, congratulate, compliment or hug to remind them how special they are.

Thank someone who opens a door for you or smiles as they hand you your change…or remind someone just how important they are to you.

Today is always a good day for a random act of kindness.

Tip#71:

Are you a generalist or a specialist?

The mind loves to learn and so we are constantly looking for more information.

Sometimes we find we have an overload or we are trying to do too many things.

We may be able to do everything to a degree, but maybe it's better to do those things that you love and have a flair for.

Finding others to do the things you struggle with allows them to follow their passions too!

Tip#72:

Notice the natural world.

Life can be easy or difficult - but do you see a bear hunting in winter, or taking time for a snooze?

Animals use nature to flow in life and we can follow if we choose.

On a full moon put your crystals out for a cleanse.

When it's raining find some indoor jobs to do.

On a sunny day spend 5 minutes soaking up sun energy. Our bodies crave flow - why fight it?

Tip#73:

What do you see?

Do you see struggle or challenge?

Do you see chaos or opportunity, do you see annoying people or potential friends?

Everything in life has two sides and two ways of looking...what are your eyes telling you?

Today see an opportunity to let the Universe do what it does, let the world turn and watch magic happen!

Tip #74:

Know your boundaries!

Who is trying to get you to bend your rules?

Who is asking you to take one step further than you are comfortable with?

If your answer is no-one, then celebrate!

If someone or a situation springs to mind, then work out what you are and are not prepared to do and watch as others respect you more.

Tip#75:

Pave your future with gold!

Every day the things you do and the actions you take pre-pave your tomorrows.

Even if you are having a day of struggles take five minutes to think of all the good things happening and all the joy you want in your future. Think of the people that make you smile and the exciting opportunities ahead.

Make that five minutes a habit and watch as a golden future unfolds.

Tip#76:

Cause confusion!

For conflict to happen there must be two people involved, one to attack, one to defend.

If someone raises a stick in attack and you don't react by raising your stick, there will be no spark to cause conflict.

This will confuse your 'opponent' and give you time to think on what to do.

Time and silence are perfect places for ingenious solutions to problems.

Tip#77:

Here is a great quote:

Obstacles are those things you see when you take your eyes off your goal.

We forget we are the creators in our lives, that we can choose how we react and where we go.

No huge effort, just consistent, tiny steps that make a chain and cause a reaction.

Spend a few moments to set your course then listen to your internal compass, it will tell you if you waiver by adding challenges.

Easy equals on course!

Tip#80:

What do you do to let your spirit play?

Do you play music, meditate or exercise, or perhaps just take five minutes out of your day to drift off in a daydream?

This allows the right side of your brain to come into play, whereas usually our left logical side is required for everyday life.

This practice will also release endorphins, calm fight or flight and give you much needed relaxation, sigh!

Tip#81:

We are great at making choices and do it every day.

Sometimes when we have a challenge or decision we only see the limiting choices, because our brain says, "Quick, you have to choose!"

Choose not to make a decision for one minute, then sit and focus on breathing, nothing else.

Feel the breath of life nourishing you and find that sense of calm.

Now play with your choices from a state of attentive calm.

Tip#78:

Look in the mirror.

Every day we look in the mirror but do we really look or does our brain just acknowledge itself and move on to the tooth brushing?

Today stop and really look, see the spark of spirit in your eyes, the face that is loved by family and friends.

Can you say 'I love and value you'?

If not say it every day for 21 days to make a habit, then watch as others around you value you more!

Tip#79:

Listen.

Have you ever been on your way somewhere and felt uneasy? Or known something was right with no outward sign?

Have you made a decision then realised you knew you were wrong?

Do you know who is draining your energy right now?

We are spirit, with great knowledge that we bring with us when we are born.

Our planet is full of distraction, but if you listen you can hear that inner guidance, gently whispering truth.

Tip#82:

Take a spa day!

While going through your normal routine add luxury to everything you do.

Focus on how cleansing your shower is, admire the beautiful spring view on your way to work.

Remember the lunch you buy is nourishing your body and relax into every conversation you have as it enriches your life in some way.

Cost: nothing.

Effect: wonderful!

Tip#83:

Celebrate!

Have you counted your blessings recently?

Celebrated all of your achievements however small: not yelling at the person that pulled in front of you, giving your child an extra hug, saying no to things you don't enjoy?

How many people have helped you recently - and how many times have you helped others?

This planet is a place for joy, celebration and loving life, if we see it that way!

Tip#84:

Create flow.

Sometimes we feel like nothing is happening and we are going nowhere.

This is never the case, as nature and life are constantly shifting like sand.

No matter how you feel always keep a positive image of the future, if you can't imagine where or how just see yourself smiling and happy.

It's also OK to ask the Universe what's next, then watch for a sign or two to show you the next step.

Tip#85:

Restore patience.

Life can be challenging, people can be frustrating and we can be impatient when in 'human' mode.

To restore spiritual functionality find a burst of energy; stand at the top of a hill and yell, or sing at the top of your voice to your favourite song.

Go for a long but pretty walk or take a sprint.

Smiling sweetly will bury your emotion; this way will get it out and allow you to start over with a genuine smile!

Tip#86:

Where do you hold your stress?

Do you tense your shoulders?

Do you forget to breathe fully?

Is your stomach in a knot or are your teeth clenched?

Our body is our shock absorber and can be moulded into our stress patterns, so give your body a treat by stretching it completely, or soaking it in a warm bath.

Perhaps take it into the sunshine, or give it heart-felt thanks for looking after you so well!

Tip#87:

Where does your energy live?

Is it spread around your body, or just between your chest and your head?

When going about our busy-ness we tend to be energy top-heavy, ignoring our lower self which can make us dizzy and confused or give us a headache.

When you take your next breath send it to your feet first, then feel it circulating your whole body, energising every cell and allowing your energy to flow freely.

Tip#88:

Are you being?

We have an ethic that we are born into to work hard and achieve, but there are many levels of work.

Being clear on your path takes a lot of work.

Being present and connected to life, paying attention and learning to choose consciously is an important step.

Taking everything on your shoulders, tiring yourself and feeling alone is also work, but something we can shrug off if we get our first step right!

Tip#89:

Think!

Every day it's good to step out of your own life and spare a thought or two for others.

Do you have friends in need of a hug that you can't get to?

Our thoughts control our mood and thoughts become things, so today send a thought out to someone in need.

Think lovingly about your family and spiritual family and enjoy that

Tip#90:

Do you believe that you are supported?

That you will never be given anything you can't deal with, that you have helpers around you and that life will sustain you with everything you need?

To not believe this breeds fear - a place of lack and more fear.

Say to yourself: 'I will always have everything I need.'

It may feel empty at first but your message will be heard and then enjoy the adventure that is life!

Tip#91:

Share.

So much goes on within us - our thoughts, our feelings, our worries. Our hopes and dreams.

Sometimes a little external influence is needed.

Writing something down allows us perspective and we can see the potential in that thought or dismiss it more easily.

If it's a dream or worry share it, encouragement has made so many people reach for the sky.

Sharing allows energy to flow and change to happen.

Tip#92:

Be you.

You are amazing, capable of anything you can imagine and more.

Be the whole you, don't compromise or hide your true self, but shine and shimmer in a glow of happy, abundant energy.

Allow happiness, ease and freedom, choose excitement and adventure.

Your only limits are those you believe to be true - and even those can change in a heartbeat!

Tip#93:

Have conversations with your body.

It sounds strange, but when you ask your body a direct question an answer appears - either a feeling or a definite answer.

When you go to bed consciously allow your body to relax, take a few minutes to think about resting your muscles and slowing your mind.

When you sit feel the support of the chair beneath you.

Little steps constantly replenish the vehicle you rely on.

Tip#94:

Use colour.

When we require boosts of energy
nature has the answer.

Our chakras are our energy centres that
absorb colour for strength.

Want to be creative? Find something
orange. Yellow for energy and self
confidence, green for more love.

Blue for self expression and clear
speech, red for feeling grounded. Violet
for intuition and pure white for
connection to spirit.

Stand outside and soak up the rainbow!

Tip#95:

Challenge the Law of Attraction!

What do you want in your life?

Is there one thing you would really, really like to happen?

Focus on that thing or event, picture it happening and feel that feeling of amazement, surprise, excitement and happiness that it's happening to you!

Then spend the rest of the day smiling as you know it's on its way!

Theories are great, but when it happens to you it's extra special!

Tip#96:

Live calmly.

Every day is filled with highs and lows; bursts of activity and periods of rest, fun bits and not so fun bits!

If too much is happening this can leave us feeling exhausted - by our activity and by our thoughts.

By going into your heart space and breathing, you will tune into the inner calm that underlies all the chaos.

Constant, supportive, peaceful and loving. Always there for you.

Tip#97:

Shine like the sun.

Wouldn't it be great to walk through today glowing with happiness, smiling at life, laughing at yourself and walking on a cushion of gold?

Where no challenge was too big, no hug too long and nothing could taint this feeling of being perfectly where you should be?

Every day this is possible, so why not start with today?

If at some point you lose the feeling, smile and start again tomorrow!

Tip#98:

What if?

Our brain loves to run scenarios…but a lot of the time it's about challenges and we think of all the things that could possibly go wrong.

Try playing an imaginary 'what if' game, where everything is possible as long as it's positive. Where colour, beauty and playfulness abound in a world full of helpers and love.

Open your eyes with a smile on your face and watch for the what ifs to become real.

Tip#99:

Be open to change.

When something doesn't go our way or plans change we can get cross and frustrated.

Sometimes it's the Universe's way of giving us a way out, or delivering something even better, so always look for the message.

Seeing lack and what you're not doing closes your world, viewing new possibilities and taking decisive action strengthens your energy and opens life up to bring in excitement and daring.

Tip#100:

Walk your talk.

We are here to learn and experience the physical, yet too often we have ideas and do nothing.

By taking one, single step towards our dream we start a process that allows miracles.

Our part is to be consistent, everything we say and do must stay in congruence so our universal helpers have a clear message and our hearts stay engaged.

Tomorrow we walk on what we say today, so make it count!

The tips in this book were channelled by Nicky, starting in January 2010. Each morning Nicky would sit quietly and tune into the words that were given to her.

To date there are now 402 tips in existence and many more to follow…

Nicky Marshall is a writer, teacher and intuitive guide.

When not at home burning pizza Nicky can be found at the coffee shop and holistic centre she created, The Witches Brew in Bristol. For details of the shop and it's services visit:

www.thewitchesbrewlimited.co.uk.

Other ways to contact Nicky:

Website: www.nickymarshall.org
E-mail: nicky@holisticinsights.co.uk
Facebook: Nicky Marshall
Twitter: nickyllmarshall

Nicky's passion is to inspire people to love their life, to celebrate the highs and to distract themselves with chocolate and good friends through the lows.

She gives readings and therapies and teaches Tarot, Reiki and Working with Energy.

Nicky is also available to facilitate workshops and give talks…as long as there is cake!

Nicky is the creator of the Love *Life!* Programme, an online resource that awakens intuition, teaches body awareness as well as relaxation, some pagan ways and personal empowerment techniques. Find the details at:

www.nickymarshall.org

Lightning Source UK Ltd.
Milton Keynes UK
UKOW041422090713

213458UK00010B/122/P